Wait a minute, God

By
Mari Rippey

Judson Press ® Valley Forge

WAIT A MINUTE, GOD

Were you ever a young mother, God?
You must know what it's like—
crying babies, soiled diapers,
skinned knees, dirty dishes, unmade
beds, interrupted schedules, delayed
meals, spilled milk, telephone calls,
sibling fights, unswept floors, muddy
feet, runny noses. Wait a minute, God,
the baby just woke up. More later.

Which is more important, Johnny or
the stew? Yes, it is a dumb question.
You have told us, God, that the whole
world is not as valuable as a person.

Then why did I get all upset?
Why did I say, "Johnny, can't you
see I'm busy and have to get supper?"

Johnny needed me and I didn't
meet his need. How many delays
and rebuffs can this child absorb
before he begins to question his
worth? How many times can I say,
"Wait till later. I've got to do this
now," before Johnny feels he is
unimportant?

Lord, help me get things in the
proper perspective. Help me keep
things in the proper perspective.
Will you, God?

It's quiet now. It's evening. All the little ones are tucked in bed. And I feel like saying, "Thank you, God."

I have nothing specific in mind. I'm thankful for things in general. Thanks for home, family, and work. Thanks for health, food, and play. Thanks for quiet moments and busy ones. Thanks for joy and laughter, but thanks for sadness and tears, too.

It's all part of your big, wide, wonderful plan. I feel comfortable knowing you are at the drawing board, God.

It's not quiet now, God. The dogs
are barking; the radio is blaring; the
traffic is buzzing by; everybody is
talking or screaming at once.

The house is utter chaos. Supper
isn't started. The day's
accomplishments seem to be nil.
Oh, the confusion!

I need you, God. I need you to
make me calm in the midst of all the
confusion. I feel like screaming,
too. Sometimes I do. Then I know
there is a better way.

Guide me into that better way.
Give me patience and peace. Give some
direction to this confusion. Will you,
God?

Your world is pretty, God. I like the sky, the grass, the trees, the wind blowing gently, the foamy seas.

But when I look closely, what is it that I see? A tiny, tiny flower. It's blue. Its petals are so even. Its yellow pistil and stamen are so tiny that I have to look closely to see them. But there they are!

You made something this beautiful, God, just for our feet to tread upon? And the green grass—softer than a carpet beneath our feet.

Yes, I hear the whispering leaves on the trees, too. I see the fluffy clouds as they scatter and come together again. It's all so beautiful, so beautiful. Thanks, God.

God, something really troubles me at times. It's the way we try to mold our children. So they will fit into our society, we tell ourselves. Or is it for our convenience? Is it to fulfill our needs?

Perhaps no reason makes it justifiable. Does this molding process squelch them? Does it inhibit their potential? Can it even ruin them?

Or is it necessary? Is it good? Is it desirable? I'm confused, God, and I need direction. How about it?

I just made my agenda for the day. It
says, "Scrub bath, make salad, sort
mail, do laundry, shine refrigerator.
. . ." And, you know, two dozen other
things.

But it doesn't say, "Pray." It
doesn't say, "Call a lonely
friend." There is no mention of
visiting my elderly neighbor or
writing a note to one who is sick.

God, how can I expect a day to be
well lived if I don't think of others?
How can I expect to get things done if I
am selfish?

Help me remember to pray.
Help me remember a friend. Help me
think of a stranger in need. May my
days always include your work
and others' needs as well as my
responsibilities.

The children view life so differently,
God. Their eyes see things in such
a fresh way.

What delight and joy they found
playing with the earthworms! What
fun they had playing in the dirt! How
excited they were when another bug
was discovered under the rock!

Help me see the fun, not the
mess, of playing in the mud. May I
share their excitement of finding
another creepy, crawly thing as they
dig.

May we as adults be able
occasionally to return to the magic
moments of life as experienced
through the eyes of a child. We
remember your words, "A little child
shall lead them."

As you know, God, I pray about
everything. It may seem silly to
other people, but, let's face it, if you
have the hairs on my head numbered,
then you are interested in
    helping Johnny cope with his
        angry feelings,
    keeping the baby from crying
        until I get supper started,
    our finding the lost keys, and
    all those other petty things that I
        pray about.
    Yes, there are more pressing
problems. Much of the world's
population is hungry. Many persons
are sick and have no doctor.
Individuals are desperately
lonely.
    But as I see it, God, you are great
enough to take care of both the big and
little needs of all of us. And at the
same time, you can keep your whole
universe running smoothly.

Do your thing, Lord. I know that you
can make the whole world go
around right. You can make my life
count.

So often I just seem to spin my
wheels. Days slip by with no
accomplishments adding up.
Weeks roll past and my good
intentions do not turn into actions.

What is it, Lord, that gives that
satisfied feeling at the end of a day?
What determines fulfillment when a
week is spent? It's that ingredient that
you add to life, isn't it? Come into
my life now, and do your thing,
Lord.

Sometimes I wonder. I wonder how
such little things can loom so large.
How can the noise of healthy
children ever disturb me? How can
a pile of laundry ever get me down?
How can I get upset because Johnny
fails to hang up his coat?

You see, God, my friend just got
home from the hospital. She had a very
serious operation. She has young
children. She has matters of life and
death to be concerned about.

How can I fret about trivia when
life is so much bigger? Forgive
me, God, and help me to get the
bigger picture. Will you?

Our son planted some seeds a few days ago. He examined the ground often. Nothing. No apparent change. Then, one day, a tender young sprout began to burst forth. How thrilling! How thrilling to see that dull, brown seed change into a green, living plant!

What was hidden in that dull, brown seed? What miracle took place as the seed died to bring forth new life?

That tiny seed tells us so much. It tells us about your plan for our lives. It tells us about the universe. And it tells us about you, God. You teach us in such fascinating ways.

It's all over, Lord. My friend, she
died—she's gone.

Just as a child asks Daddy why
the sun sets, I need to ask you, "Why?"

Even though I may not
understand your ultimate plan, help
me accept it. Assure me that everything
will work for good.

Help me see more fully how
death is a part of life. How death is
just another step to take—another
door to open—another discovery to
make.

It's the beginning of a new day. In fact,
it's the beginning of a new week.

I have all these grandiose plans. I'll
clean my closet. I'll read extra books
to Johnny. I'll write a letter. And the
clutter—I'll not let it appear. I'll keep
the house neat as we go along. I'll
mend the baby's sleepers. I'll have
supper ready on time. I'll take time
to talk with the children and do the
things they want to do.

Oh, I'm so full of enthusiasm.
Help me keep it, God.

Thanks for our toddler. As I rocked him in my arms tonight, I cried a tear or two. They were tears of love, thankfulness, and appreciation.

People say the years go quickly by. I don't see things from this perspective when he is a "terrible two." But I did tonight. I realized that someday he would be grown up. That I could no longer rock him in my arms.

I truly enjoyed him these moments tonight. Why don't I do it more often? Thanks for toddlers, God.

This committee! That project! That
drive! Volunteer one hour! Could
you make these calls? Would you
serve on this task force? Can you help
your church? Your school? Your
community?

Lord, what about my family?
I feel guilty when I say no to all the
requests. But I feel more guilty when I
find the things I say yes to requiring
so much of my time that the family
suffers.

The church needed telephone
callers. "When will you be off the
phone?" Johnny whines. They
asked that I write an article for the
newsletter. "When can you stop
writing and read me a book?" was the
request from the toddler at my
knee.

Lord, give me guidance in
setting priorities. Help me be fair to
my church, the school, the
community. But most of all, help me
be fair to my family.

It's a bright, beautiful, sunny day.
WOW, do I want to thank you for
it!

All that energy that the tots
have had stored up during the rainy
days can be released. They can run.
They can jump. They can climb
the apple tree. They can play ball.

It's great for them. It's great for
me. And I just wanted you to know,
God, I appreciate your sending this
beautiful day.

Hey, God, I really need your help
with this decision. I've tossed it
about so long, and I'm tired of the
agony of indecision.

I have examined all sides,
considered all possibilities, and am so
uncertain. Could you just throw a
little light on the whole problem?
Maybe you could even open a door
or toss me a new thought about it.

Please guide me, God.

I grumbled about that pile of laundry.
I grumbled about sorting it and the
trips upstairs and downstairs to load
and unload the washer and dryer.

Then I stopped and considered. I
have an automatic washer. I push
a button for cold or hot water. I have
a dryer. How can I grumble?

What if I had to carry the water,
heat the water, make my soap,
scrub on the washboard, and dry the
clothes on the grass? Or what if we had
no clothes to wash?

How can I grumble? Forgive me,
Lord. May I have love and
compassion for those who have no
washer and dryer.

Sometimes I enjoy doing the dishes.
Yes, sometimes it is even inviting to
have a few dishes soaking in hot,
sudsy water.

But tonight, Lord, it's bedtime
and I'm sleepy; but there they are—
dirty dishes everywhere. There are
dirty dishes in the sink, on the stove, and
on the counter. Some are soaking in
cold, grimy water. They are not inviting
tonight.

Can you perform a miracle just
now and make me enthusiastic about
doing all those dirty dishes? Can you,
Lord?

Sometimes things are so grand.
Life seems good and full and
satisfying. That's when we have good
rapport—with you, with our
families, with our friends. That's when
we are satisfied with ourselves. That's
when we've realized a portion of our
potential. It's when we have lived as
you said, Lord, loving you first and
our neighbor as ourselves.

Thank you for these times when
we feel like all is well and when
we feel in tune.

Thanks for the satisfaction that
comes from kneading this dough.
Thanks for the smiles and cries of
delight that will come from my
family when I carry the plate of hot
cinnamon buns to the table.

We all need fulfillment and
satisfaction and success. And isn't it
funny that these feelings only come
when we are doing for others? This
helps us understand, Lord, what
life is all about.

Creator, where is your creation? I
haven't been out of this house today.
Sure I could have put boots, mittens,
sweaters, hats, and coats on the kids
and gone for a walk.

It's such an effort. It seemed
easier to stay inside. It seemed easier
to face the blare of the television and
the clutter of toys.

But I really have no excuse,
do I? For all of our sakes we should
have put on our boots and walked in
the half-frozen, muddy grass and felt
the warmth of your winter sun on our
backs.

Maybe tomorrow we can. Yes,
Lord, thanks for the promise of
tomorrow.

A red cardinal!
It's sitting in our crab apple tree. I
can see it from our kitchen window.
Indeed, God, it is beautiful! Thank
you for making cardinals. Thank
you for letting this cardinal come
and brighten my day. May I serve you
in the same way—by helping to
brighten someone's day.

Oh, do I need you, God! I need you now. I feel buried. I feel down under—
emotionally, physically,
spiritually.

Could you offer me just a ray of light? Could you spare some encouragement for me right now? Could you at least help me to think positively?

God, you know just telling you about it helped. Thanks, thanks so much for listening.

It's Friday. Thank you for making
Fridays. Not that things will change
that much. There are still meals to
cook, diapers to change, floors to
sweep. But the little changes that come
are so welcome.

Things like our family
eating Saturday morning breakfast
together. And painting a room
together. The whole family having a
little football scrimmage. Going to
church. Taking a walk to hear the
leaves rustle under our feet. Popping
popcorn over the fire in the
fireplace.

Thanks for Fridays because
they step into weekends, and that is
when these special things happen.

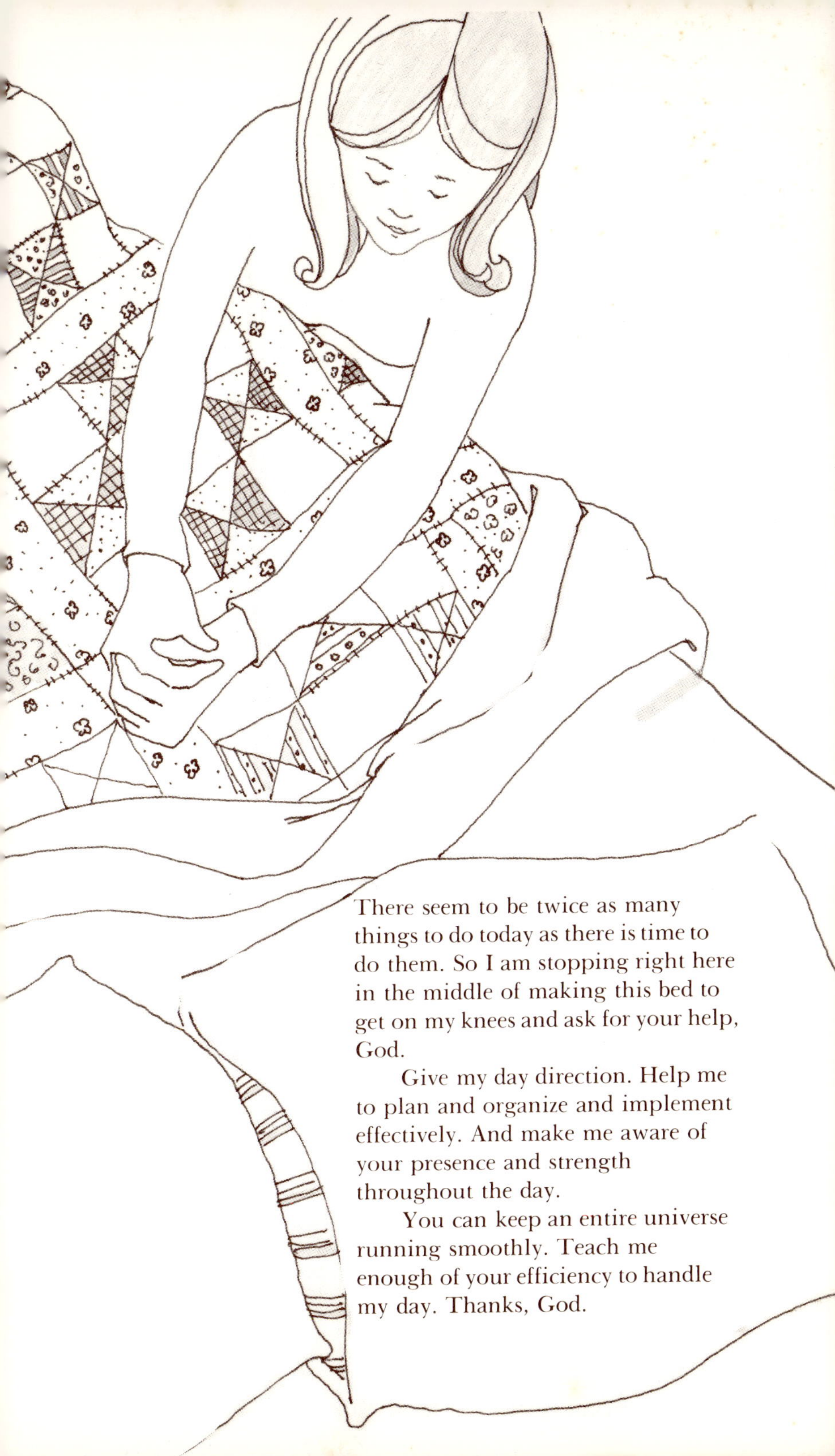

There seem to be twice as many things to do today as there is time to do them. So I am stopping right here in the middle of making this bed to get on my knees and ask for your help, God.

Give my day direction. Help me to plan and organize and implement effectively. And make me aware of your presence and strength throughout the day.

You can keep an entire universe running smoothly. Teach me enough of your efficiency to handle my day. Thanks, God.

Oh, does this bed feel good tonight,
God! How can you ask me to get on my
knees and pray when I'm so tired?

Oh, you didn't ask me? Where did I
get that idea? Now I know. I want to
be on my knees. Otherwise, I'd go to
sleep and not pray.

But I want to pray. I want to say
thanks. I want to thank you for
tiredness and refreshing sleep. I
want to thank you for my family, for
love, for the universe, for you. Yes,
just thanks, Lord.

Lord, you must know how frustrated
we become sometimes with the
challenges of parenthood.

When the children come to me, it is
so easy to nod a yes or mumble,
"Uh-huh," without ever knowing really
what they said. I continue my
dusting, wishing they wouldn't
interrupt as I try to do household
duties.

Lord, when the children come to
me, let me be excited, not irritated with
them. Help me be patient as they try
hard to express their thoughts in their
childish language. Let me share
their enthusiasm about the little
things in life. Help me really to listen
to what they have to say.

"This little piggy went to market,
this little piggy stayed home. . . ."

Our baby giggles with delight as
Daddy finds each little toe and recites
the familiar rhyme. Thank you, God,
for the tiny toes and the giggles of
delight.

Thank you for all the magic
moments of growing up. We saw
the miracle of birth. We delighted in
the first smile. We helped steady the
first faltering steps. We kissed the
skinned knees. We were thrilled
with the first "Da-Da."

Thank you for all the special
moments. Thank you for the
privilege of sharing life with children.
Yes, thanks!